What We Have To Live With

also by Marilyn Krysl

Poetry:
Saying Things (Abattoir Editions)
More Palomino, Please, More Fuchsia (Cleveland State Poetry Center)
Diana Lucifera (Shameless Hussy Press)
Midwife and Other Poems on Caring (National League for Nursing)

Stories:
Honey, You've Been Dealt A Winning Hand (Capra Press)
Mozart, Westmoreland and Me (Thunder's Mouth Press)

What We Have To Live With

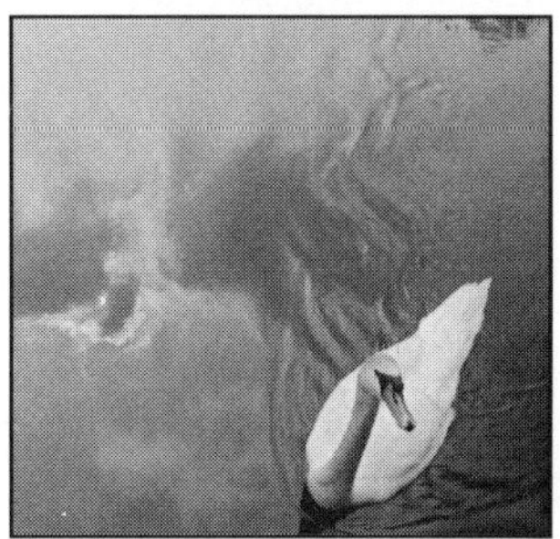

Marilyn Krysl

TEAL PRESS
Santa Fe, New Mexico

For Riva

Some of these poems have appeared in the following publications:

Another Chicago Magazine: "Spell", "The Back"; *Denver Quarterly*: "Peoples' Republic Of China: The No. 1 Machine Tool Factory Foreman's Wife", "Peoples' Republic of China: The Open Ended Sestina", "West Lake, Hangzhou", "Sestina Rima: She Laments Her Rotten Luck"; *Field*: "Leda"; *Helicon Nine*: "Six", "Reciprocal"; *High Plains Literary Review*: "Matriphobia"; *Indiana Review*: "Drawing"; *Iowa Review*: "September, You Remember The Ottoman Empire", "Thermodynamics"; *Kansas Quarterly*: "The Beautiful Alive Alone Illusion", "Venus", "Passage"; *Open Places*: "The Foreign Woman Applauds The Failure Of Ideal Systems", "Are You The Malthus Ma Or The Marxist Ma?", "Snapshot, Tianjin, 1982: The Extended Sestina"; *Prairie Schooner*: "Grandmother", "Talking All Night"; *The Little Magazine*: "Sestina Against Matrimony", "Persephone, To Demeter", "O.K., I'll Tell You"; *The Nation*: "Demeter", "Two Women"; *The Eleventh Muse*: "Incarnate"; *13th Moon*: "Red Embroidered Shoes".

Some of these poems, "Silverware", "Poem At 5:05 In The Morning", "The Muse And Her Instrument", "*Pas Seul*", "Two Women", "Navel", "Dreams From War", and "Body", also appeared in *Saying Things* by Marilyn Thompson, issued in a limited edition by Abattoir Editions, University of Nebraska Press, Omaha, 1975.

First Edition

Printed in the United States of America

Library of Congress Cataloging-in-Publication Data

Krysl, Marilyn, 1942-
What we have to live with / Marilyn Krysl. — 1st ed.
p. cm.
ISBN 0-913793-12-4 (alk. paper): $7.00
I. Title.
PS3561.R88W47 1989
811'.54—dc20 89-20191
CIP

A Teal Press Poetry Series Book
Book Design: Robert Jebb
Typographics: Copygraphics, Inc., Santa Fe, New Mexico
Teal Press books are Smyth sewn for durability and printed on acid-free paper for longevity.

Teal Press
P.O. Box 4098
Santa Fe, New Mexico 87502

Contents

West Lake, Hangzhou

Is that Bach? Is this evening? Isn't Bach blue, isn't
the lake lovely. In this heat. The air
above the water almost steams. Those boats
go slower. Dusk, one long swatch of chamber
music, laid across water. If there's a better
way, we haven't found it. Standing, burning,

here on the balcony, you discover you're happy. The burning
lotus blossoms light the lake. Isn't
this evening blue beyond belief? Better
than being in love is being here, in love. The air
holds still, giving us sweet time: a chamber
maid tinkling keys in the hall. Those boats

are nothing if not beautiful. A scattering of boats
completes a lake, your hand completes my burning
shoulder. Say the charge enters the chamber,
fills the space to bursting. Some will say this isn't
so, lake not lovely, light and air
less than crystal clear. Doubters. (Better

to die, get it over.) Where could be better
than here: the mosquitoes don't bite (it's true!), boats
have no motors. The dip of oars and a Bach aire
riffling my blood. Leaves of the banana burning
like beaten brass in my fortieth year. Isn't
this the body the gods intended? The chamber

where they lie down with us? Listen: in the chamber
of the ear, a continuous tune! (If there's a better
restaurant, we'll find it tonight.) The question isn't
when, but how good can it get. Say we let the boats
decide, flung white stones of *I Ching*: burn
of the day in our blood, the lotus closing, air

lifting like swallows joined at the wing, the air
beginning to cool, lights coming on, chamber
music (not bad!) somewhere below us, and the burning
bridge behind. Doing it's always better
than not. Afterward you go on, and where there are boats
who needs a bridge? What good's a shoulder, if it isn't

burning? Isn't the chamber of a lover's arms
blue beyond belief? Isn't a hexagram
of boats, afloat on air, better even than Bach?

Six

My daughter wears a watch
today, perched on her wrist
like a wren. Waiting
for the bus, I ask her
the time. She consults
this oracular bird at
length: thirty-seven
minutes to eleven.

September, You Remember The Ottoman Empire

Days like this you remember grade school, the smell
of pencils, the hot, whirring drone of the clock
as you brought forth the names of the great metals:
platinum, zinc, manganese, copper, silver,
gold, mercury, chromite, vanadium, tin.
Antimony was important in peace and war.
The core of the earth was liquid nickel and iron

and fact was muscle. You were bigger than anybody.
You could have walked all the way to Duluth
for a start. Whole zones of the earth as yet
unmarked by your boot: Tibet and the tundra—
that rug over Russia—jungle, savannah, glacier,
the moon. You were capable of just about probably
everything. The teacher sat alone at the end

of the room. So it was decided: you would go
among the great populations. Tokyo six million
then. Africa shimmering with tribes. Tanzania,
Chile, Bolivia, Guam. The whole Chinese nation
starving and teeming. Arabians in silver tents
against the desert storm. The invention of the knout.
The Slavs and their snows.

                                             In Ohio there is
no history. Beside you Harrold Gene
was chewing gum. He was fat, and dumb. You were
thirteen. How you ached to get into history:
Jesus, Mohammed, Eisenhower, Churchill, the Queen.

Body

My body is too many children, they are all hungry at once. As I write this one of them bangs my thigh with a doll. I say, *Stop that!* But my body is headstrong. When it doesn't get its way it throws a tantrum. Once it kicked a wall and broke three toes. In winter it sulks because it can't go swimming. Good days it sits and pouts because it can't fly. And some days it won't put on its clothes no matter where we're going. It gets oily and sweats and sits in its mess, breathing, and I have to wash and comb it patiently and sing it little songs, and then it goes to the party

without me. I come later, alone. I tell it it's going to regret all that *beaujolais.* But my body is defiant, has another glass, and another, gets roaring. The next afternoon I have to phone and apologize. I say, *Please excuse my body. There is no excuse for its conduct, but now it regrets the greedy gobbling of hors d'oeuvres, those lies about your gracious wife.* Then I march it to the mirror in the bathroom and I make myself stern and say sharply, *I'm ashamed of you! When are you going to grow up?* And my body hangs its head. But I'm suspicious. Should I trust it?

When we have a dentist appointment my body hangs back. I am cheery. *Be brave,* I tell it. But my body is nervous, makes excuses. Then I have to say, *At your age! This is disgraceful!* It starts to sniffle, to grovel, to beg. *If only,* it says. In the end I drag it to the car. Slam the door and rev the motor. *Some day I'll wash my hands of you,* I say.

Then one night it sits down on the bed, strokes the cat. Is anything wrong? The cat jumps off, my body lies down, stares at the ceiling. And now I understand that it is sad. The other body it wants to be loved by has flown off to Bermuda with the redhaired stewardess, and now my body says it wants to die. So I sit down beside it. *Wouldn't you like to go for a walk?* I ask. *Shall I get you a glass of cold water? Want me to brush you hair?* But it turns away. Is it weeping?

It is weeping. Now its eyes are red, its face splotched, it is ugly. What can I say—it gives me pleasure and grief, and now it is weary, so heavy, its face sags, it doesn't care about the mirror anymore. It doesn't care about the public or about politics. It doesn't love music or admire the plastic arts. It is tired, it has stopped pretending. I will go out quietly and let it sleep.

Dreams From War

Men, bloody, approach the house
from the trees. One, two, strayed
from the war, they have been wandering
the forest, looking for their death.
In the deaths of so many
others their own death eludes them.

Earlier some grass beside a stream
seemed like a woman's hair. *Hush, hush,*
like skirts, the branches of firs. What this
reminds them of these men do not now
remember. The kisses of women have dried,
flaked from their lips. Isn't that a
fox on the path, glimpsed through snow?

Maybe the house is sleep. It is white,
steam on the panes. Something ordinary, a broom
left by the step, the owner abroad. On the table
part of a loaf. Now the men are dizzy.
In a half loaf of bread a man can sleep
without regrets. Wet flakes, whirling
softly, bits of white cake. In the woods
they gnawed the inner bark of saplings.

Their weariness is pure,
like snow. By it they intend
nothing. But maybe the house is a trap?
Is a pie cooling on the sill?

Far to the south children sleep in the beds
with their mothers. The women stroke the children
like little cats. Fuzz gathers on the floor.
Hibiscus float in glass bowls. The women doze
endlessly. Yards are lush, untrimmed,
empty. The hum of the gas heater
steady. The women's dreams are gray,

old pillows ripped open.
In the tissue paper stories they read to the children
bears wear suits and silk hose.

Sestina Against Matrimony

No, I will not marry. I will be merry. Thank you
no thank you. This burial
for the common wealth is not musical,
believe me. One for the price of two
is a net loss
of one, Locke be damned, and I am more solitary

than the two armed couplet can hold. In solitary
is fresh air, *cantabile.* More sestinas, thank you,
these things take room. There is no loss
worse than the burial
of the spacious self. Give me a room for two
with a view and I will show you the musical

possible. Impossible, this ponderous musical
by Wagner! I prefer the light solitary
and me, trumpeting airily into the great dark. Two
dolls, mechanistic antiphonal, no, no thank you.
The couplet is soon ding dong, a Sousa march to the burial
grounds, a gradual *diminuendo a deux.* Loss

of gaiety for piety is loss
far from tuneful, and I am by nature musical
and plenty of me. To double is to stifle, and burial
is the coroner's business. I will aria from the solitary
balcony where there is air to hear me out. Thank you,
yes, I'll have two

sestinas, here where the air is cold. Two
crowds the tiny couplet, and it reads DOUBLE LOSS,
MINUS GAIN. The answer is no, no, no thank you, no.
One sestina takes a page, and music
fills the lush, spreading solitary
until it spills over. You must be dead to be buried.

But the nuptial looks very like a burial!
Do not Juliet me. The first apes (and note there were two
of them) pell mell out of tropical solitary
into double jeopardy. Loss
of the spheres for a polka! Believe me, there's nothing musical
in two chairs, straightbacked, side by side. No thank you,

Lohengrin's two certificates of burial for the nomadic, monodic,
musical phrase. Solitary's not confinement, it's grand opera
and I have not lost my voicc. Good night, I go my ways.

Talking All Night
for Peter

Near dawn the whirr of our talk,
that edge of white brine,
thins down. We

yawn,
          I settle in along
your side, feel you

let go. You
who were wound,
                                        hemp
on a winch driving a pulley,

lie at last long and sonorous,

bell peal
subsiding beside me.

Persephone, To Demeter

Mother, I'll
tell you. Let me tell you it's
easy, going down in the
dark. I take all the right drugs,
not too much, not too little, I'm

    careful. I count the stone
        steps: one at a
            time. Each step taking me

deeper, my feet
    repeating, and I listen
        to my breathing, the piston
            thrust, back and forth,

of my breath. My fingertips
    pull along the stone
        wall. It's something to
            feel. Then I see the first star

for the last time. I look down
for good. The seconds iron links
I am forging, making a vast mail,
a chain, and there isn't any
pain: Mother, it feels like

nothing at all. I proceed at a steady
crawl, each step a dull
thud. I have your iron
in my blood. And soon enough

I arrive. He asks after
your health, takes my hand like a father, a distant
brother. Mother, there's not much
to eat, but down here I don't
care. No fruit, a thin, red
wine. A white
bed. I

sleep. The rest
is easy. You know the rest. I'm
not allowed out, I may not
seem busy. No knitting, no purling,
no throwing myself into the
piano, there

isn't one. I pass time in the same
room with him, stare at the wall,
let him think I'm thinking of
him. A tight schedule of silence,
punctual meals. Waiting it out,

biting my nails. Mother,
listen: it's coming back that isn't
easy. There's nothing worse than having to
retrace memory. Erase
iron. I have to

erase iron: think of it, Mother,
trying to pry loose all the little
links in the blood, one at a time, and climb

uphill, carrying my own image,
his gift to you and yours
to him:
            a daughter, the reminder
that this is hell
the two of you made
together. I am
the struck bargain, the go
between. I go

between the narrow walls, up the damp
stairs, not a spiral but straight up,
and I sweat, approaching your heat,
I hear water, laughter, the piano
and you. Mother, it

hurts. It hurts to be your
daughter, I didn't know if I could
do it, I thought I might
die, aching toward
your voice, calling *summer, come here*
        summer,
                my foot on the next to the last
                    tread—and then you said

daughter.
            Daughter, you say,
standing in the lighted
doorway, letting the scissors
fall from your hand. Mother, it

hurts,
pulled up into
scalding light, it hurts to look
in your eyes again, to get
well again, to keep
climbing up out of hell again

and again. Mother, it hurts
the way the foot, unbound, rips apart
as the blood, streaming back,
screams down its track. Mother,
I tell you, it hurts. But Mother,

I'm back.

The Back

for Elizabeth

Because all day we face front, and in the evening
sit facing each other across a table, and even
if there are many of us, the back like a coat
thrown over a chair is out in the cold. Because

when you look at the naked back you think of the very
young and their helpless trusting, because you can't
not think of the very old. For these reasons,
because the back is the loneliest part of the body

when you reach for me you reach around me.
My shoulderblades close like eyelids closing in ecstasy
and the back, mute with neglect, begins to stutter
oh please, yes, please do that, and you do:

erect under your hands like pile in velvet,
like hundreds of faces almost beginning to smile,
like the face of the prisoner just released from isolation
coming toward you at last up the long corridor,

walking in a way that tells you you are responsible now,
you will have to make long, slow love to her, and quickly,
because she has forgotten there is love in the world
and she will not be able to remember alone.

Reciprocal

You come in your nightgown, clutching the small, sweaty
bouquet of your worries: fifteen pages every night
and you're not a fast reader. Draw a map of California,
how high is the Matterhorn, Genghis Khan, who is he—

all by tomorrow! The teacher writes *fabulous* across
your subtraction, but you're not convinced. Twilight is ruined.
And gym three times a week—an outrage, you will write
to the President. You are sorry, but it will not be possible

ever to do the dishes again.
I take your
flowers, my vase fills with evening. A new moon
rests on the rim. We spell *magnitude* while it goes
down. I pull back the sheet, part your hair straight:
there. A glass of milk. I fill

as you drink.

Navel

Your lover kisses you there, but now
it won't open like the mouth
it once was. It's the place where the surgeon,
a stern father, yelled "That's enough!"
and deft as a killer, twisted the noose
into a bow knot
and cinched it shut.

Or was it your mother, trapped between fear
and love, who wheeled, snarling, and with her canines
cut you off. You were half a kiss
ripped from its other half
and the blood a thin, red scream,
goodby, goodby, goodby,

and you closed. The wound
healed. Now that scar's the insignia
of your isolation. Neat as a stamp, it should be
gold leaf, certified—successful completion of one way
rite de passage. Once a passageway,
now a plug. Intact as a button, stuck there
to remind you you're stuck here, you can't
get out and you can't crawl back inside
mother, and no one can enter you either, you're

sealed. The letter's mailed. You've been
stoppered, the cork's
grown to the bottle, now if you want to
talk you've got to use
words. Look, it's the end of a bolt
sunk in its lock. Someone said,
"Shut up your crying!"
and that's where they stuffed the gag.

The Beautiful Alive Alone Illusion

I do not feel beautiful
in the black dress. In the white dress
I felt beautiful when I met you
and you too
were wearing white. But I don't feel
that I alone, in a vacuum,

am beautiful. Oh I do,
but it seems a lonesome, a
vacuous beauty. When I walked
through the hotel lobby toward you
I heard the boy at the desk say *Jesus,*
BEAUTIFUL! I thought
it was our meeting
he was remarking. It
wasn't, but he was

wrong. Because the solitary figure
at the top of those stairs
is fake. The figure
is a prop in an ad
for Chrysler. A woman
in a silver dress
about to own a car
of her own, drive it herself
down a long strip of asphalt
called a freeway. What they
don't tell you

is that she will never
drive it anywhere,
this woman in silver, a Chrysler
at her feet. If only

she could. She might drive
alone, long
distances. She might
meet a mechanic, or get her hands
greasy checking the oil herself,
she might even get grease
on her dress. "What a
mess!" she'd say, wink at the attendant,
and drive on.

She might even
fall asleep at the wheel,
smash right into a Subaru
and die. Even people driving Chryslers
do.

And she might discover
she's not beautiful, even in a silver dress
in a Chrysler

because she's alone in the Chrysler
and the Chrysler
doesn't care.

No one is beautiful
dead. No one is beautiful alive
and alone. No one is beautiful
alone, even in silver
at the top. That's an illusion
that may sell a lot of women
Chryslers
but it *is* an illusion
and illusions aren't beautiful
because they're not

real. So when I put on the lavender and burgundy
dress and stand at the mirror
I observe that although I look
sexy daring delicious vogue arresting
and chic

I am not beautiful. But I am
excited, keyed up, and just a little bit jittery
because I'm alive
and about to go down the stairs
to the lobby and across

just as you enter
from the opposite side.

The Foreign Woman Applauds The Failure Of Ideal Systems

What am I doing here, in the land of purity?
Marxism-Leninism-Mao-Tse-Tung-Thought is worse
than the Bible. A system this idealistic is asking
for trouble, The People sure to fall short: *guilty,*
guilty! Then wreak what havoc guilt brings on.
There is only one Mao, there is only one St. Paul.

As a kid, and devout, I admired him greatly, St. Paul,
but I knew I'd stay deep in the clay, purity
several stories above me. Mao said, "We're here. Bring on
the Revolution." I don't know which is worse:
the Status Quo or Progress. Certainly guilt's
predictable. The inscrutable Chinese bow, then ask

the impossible. And of each other. I'd ask
you over, but here a Strauss waltz is evil. Mao's
method's marriage, til death do us part: a gilt
coach for a man who admired female purity
the way Catholics admire the foetus. What's worse
the woman's feared. Here she comes now, bringing on

musical plagues! Top button open! (Bring on
the porn.) Watch out, the next thing you know she'll ask
you to dance. And she likes it—what could be worse!
"It is good for a man not to touch a woman." St. Paul
lecturing the Corinthians. "Nevertheless, to avoid impurity
let every man have his own wife." Guilt

was thus absolved all neatly—and thus the guilty
acquired (without seeming to) property. Mao brings on
a similar rhetoric: loaded, but empty. Purity,
a "custom" for the last six centuries (ask
Mary Daly), don't give up easy. St. Paul
would approve this Communist Paradise, no worse

no better, than before Liberation. Though much the worse
for me, all hot and rank and steamy—guilty
of curiosity. "Your glorying is not good." St. Paul
again, a din of accusations. (Bring on
the aspirin, I'm giving him a headache.) "Woman, you ask
too much!" Mao and St. Paul acapella. Purity

come down from Christ and Confucius. Communists or Christians,
which, I ask you, is worse. Keep your purity,
fellas, and bring on that Presley. I'd rather be guilty.

Pas Seul

Midnight. The house
a hull. The children smooth in their beds,
their breath water,
and I sit at last at the silver mirror,

brush my hair. Behind me the bed,
a slab of moonlight, and the brush
      whispering in my ear,
systole, diastole, systole, diastole, each stroke
a second, a year,
      and behind the mirror
that animal whose eyes are black holes

waits. Patient.
A dog, its great head
nodding with the brush.

But I too am patient. Let it wait.

O.K., I'll Tell You

I carried you abroad in the world

of my excellent body. I moved
about, the sea inside me
rocked. Mornings

when the waters were
stirred up, I planted
olive trees to hold the earth
steady. By one I was
done, the sea
calm. I slept

all afternoon. Then
dusk, back again
in society. Your father, the clink
of silver, voices from the neighbor's
patio. The phone. The news. Gin,
and the sunset. I was young: all this
would simply go on.

One evening we went for a walk
on the golf course. Back, reading
a magazine, I felt the snap
of waters pulling apart—
that sound the Red Sea made for Moses—

and by God I was back in the Old
Testament, a book I supposed
I'd closed for good when I
slammed the door of my parents'
house. (That's how neat
I thought things could be
done up.) THE LORD THY GOD
IS A JEALOUS GOD: flat
on my back, about to become
great, I understood at last
that statement.

So the long dinner party
was over. The middle class, I supposed,
would go on for some. Those Buicks,
all that ease, the alcoholic twilights.
The women endlessly receptive, the men
endlessly there.

Your father
stood on the bank, wondering
what on earth had got into me.
There was no such thing

as society: there were
the towering waters

and me. And me, I was about to

deliver. On the other side,
if I made it, the busy land
of milk and honey. Cows
and bees. My breasts began
to rise to the occasion,
and I thought I would probably
never sleep again

I'd be so busy
running the new world.

Venus

Heat of orchids
in her breasts, sun
                                        a glistening animal

on her shoulder. This
is the jungle. This is the jungle
of the senses, brilliant

the toucan of the throat.
Go on, and a stream
fondles itself

beneath the lime trees. Kneel,
drink from the small spring. Her
waist through trees

a view of savannahs. Those who walk
the humus path, who walk here
amidst her lights and shadows
will decide against dying.

Two Women

Over the soft, white bread I begin to cry
salt, these thin
shoes, old coat, a few friends
        far from me
as though I flung them in disgust.

In me this dark
squall of winter, over the house wraith of winter,
and I cannot see beyond my sleepless wrath
and winter, my daughter without
father,
and now water
drips into a pan
in the room where she sleeps her perfect
dreamless sleep.

Genealogy

for Riva

My daughter is sewing, a sound like mowing
in the distance. As she leans
over this field of white cotton, feeding
the cloth through, I can see that's the way
my mother sits, sewing, leaning forward.
My daughter's back is my mother's back
but smaller. Already my daughter is
my size, and though she may never be as tall
as my mother, her hands are larger now
than my hands. I can feel her moving out
in front of me, the way in the next lane,
little by little, a runner gains and begins
to pull ahead. As she sews I swear I see
her advance, headed for that final stretch

my mother won't reach. I have always been
the smallest in my family. And I will have shrunk,
the way the old do. My daughter will hum, sewing
the ripped seam in my dress, talking
and filling me in as she helps me
back into it. I'll look around for my
cane, not see it: carefully
sit back down. She'll find it fallen
beside the chair and say "Here," easing me
up, patient with my progress, as I am not
patient. I'll be pissed off at my own
doddering, my damned slowness, and I will
rap at each step with as much wrath
as I can muster, to let the world know
I'm not accepting this state of affairs,

not yet. I'll mutter things, things an old woman
shouldn't say to her daughter. "Oh Mother,"
she'll say, laughing, laying her hand on my
shoulder. And her hand, there,

will be the large, sure hand of my mother.

Sea Legs

Brandy burns in the glass. Thank god
for drink. What we thought was the bed
turns into a boat, and now here comes

the ocean. (And we thought we'd discovered
a continent. Mountains, plains, gravity,
cocktails.
               Trusting, we took off
our clothes. There would be game,
friendly tribes. We intended

to plant potatoes. In due time
furnishings, paintings
on the walls. A chair to lay
my blouse across. Love,
                                   we agreed,
is a solid. So I let my pony tail
down.)

               Did I say
paintings? I'll never see
that blouse again. One wall
is yellow, and there it goes,
opening onto the open

sea! Quick, we'd better drink
some more of this. This is the
ocean we're on, friend,
                                   and out here,

out here we will eat Sargasso
or die.

O.K., all right, so it isn't
granite. But notice how gulls
glide down, extending
directions. How the water

brightens
as the shoreline
recedes. Here, have the last
swallow. Liquidities,

after all, have a certain
allure,
and when there are
no certainties, love becomes

water you can walk on.

Leda

A man
isn't
a swan. A man isn't a calculator
either, even if he does make phone calls and memos
at a desk. A man isn't a man at a
desk and a man at a desk isn't a father,
the broken lake isn't his daughter,
and the only woman in a cluster of men
isn't a man.

                    When the maps
are finished, she won't tell you what to do.
He's not your keeper. This isn't a halfway
house, a home, a security blanket or a kettle
of fish. Mary isn't his mother, Shakespeare
isn't a man. This isn't a manual. A woman
isn't a mixing vessel, and he isn't outside
looking in. This isn't a sonnet and it isn't
easy. You're not a fake and I'm not
faking. Tasting alone won't tell us
if the water's pure.

                    I can't be
                              encouraging.
I won't urge you to make yourself useful.
The artist isn't an answering service, and
she's not a physical therapist. A behaviorist
isn't a man, God isn't a woman. I didn't
install the electric fence, you didn't invent
the cattle prod. God
isn't black either. He didn't deliver the missing
piece, instructions for dismantling
didn't come with it, and while you were out

there was no mail. She didn't come. A cow
isn't a woman. This isn't the letter she
didn't leave, or a red flag. A man's not a bull
or a goat. Or a sheep. We're not lambs, this
isn't the slaughterhouse. If you need directions
to the party, make them up. This isn't Hollywood
calling. I didn't answer the phone. Hollywood
isn't calling, the phone didn't ring. And the
phone isn't ringing now. Why are you waiting,
why are you still expecting a phonecall?

Spell

My child has a headache. I say
come here. Lie down. Put my hands
in her hair. The hair of a child
is brighter than new leaves

and gives off heat. My hands
recite, they repeat the old
rhymes, the tinny din of busyness
runs down. I can hear

again. I can hear the hum
of her hair, that high of a thin
string, the body's colors
spinning beneath her skin,

feel the air in the room
ring, grain of the threshold
swell, the philodendron dense
with chlorophyll, the pillow

beneath her head filling with light

and in that vast space inside
my fingertips, the particles
streaming, and my daughter falling
asleep. I have made peace

and it will rise. Many and multiple
our ancient properties, and first
among these the galactic fingers'
span. We have always been

good with our hands.

Are You The Malthus Ma Or The Marxist Ma?

The tall tree breaks in the wind. So said
the sage. No tall trees here. Here the masses
prevail, a uniform blue. One mass. *Many*
is putting it mildly. Ma Ying Tsu walked the endless
boulevards past the day nurseries. The Great Helmsman
believed in the family. Ma Ying Tsu said, "Imagine

all China like Tokyo, like New Delhi. Imagine
a person who's never been alone. Confucius said,
I looked toward Kuan Pass: there was no man
in Kuan. That was B.C. Overpopulation means endless
production. And they could turn against you." (How did so many

emperors hold on so long?) He'd lived this many
years in two rooms with nine others. A mathematician, he imagined
a room of his own, a view of a valley, endless
distance. "I can't turn around," Brave Orchid said,
"and not touch somebody." Hell's another baby. And the mass,
in China, is more than the sum of its parts. This man

could figure. They climbed the rostrum. "Comrade Chairman,
take Malthus. A barbarian, but he was clever. Too many
Marxists multiplying could mean an uprising." The masses
filled Tian An Men Square. Ma Ying Tsu imagined
Peking woman needling her man. She said,
"I've had it with this crowd, these kids, the endless

debating the merits of Marxism-Leninism, the endlessly
repeating rhetoric. I'm starving. Let's split." A man,
Mao loved a crowd at his feet. "Relax," he said,
"enjoy the view." The Square blue, many
red flags, bicycles, couples with babies. He imagined
more, this Chairman. He had a vision: masses

of tall trees bending low in the wind. "The masses
bend and bend and do not break." Endless
resilience is very Chinese. Or is it? "Imagine
a woman," Ma Ying Tsu argued. "Two babies. Imagine a woman,
one babe at each breast, millions of women, many
more children, children to the horizon." He said,

"Mao, for the masses' sake, use your imagination!
Heaven may be many women, pregnant, in blue.
Hell is their kids," he said, "in endless queue."

*(Mao ignored the advice of Ma Ying Tsu, who was
China's Malthus. The poem's title is a remark
Mao is reputed to have addressed to Ma.)*

Thermodynamics

We sit, holding hands. The brightness of things
hurts. Metal's ineffectual. A bus shimmers
and breaks down. All of the children are out
working the swimming pools. A bike, tipped,

melts in the street. Conversation is out of the
question. The heat is soft force (yes,
take off my dress), one by one lifting
the lids of the molecules, so that you can hear them

tick. Listen: the table. Plates in a stack.
The phone. That brass bowl has petals unfolding.
Now the far off, flowering peal of a bell.
Even the dog's becoming flora. And we will

too. Because of the molecules. Because your teeth
want to talk to my shoulder. Because the core
of the earth is liquid nickel and iron, you know
I did not come here to be alone,

and the Mayor's declared the afternoon off. Lie
down. Think of my belly as a celebration.
Think of the fact that we're made mostly of water.
Think of your tongue as a song to a lake in the sun.

Now think of the ocean, the remains of those shellfish
over the centuries becoming the oil we burn
for heat. And you and I a field of grain getting taller,
oats, soybeans, sugarbeets, rye grass, wheat.

Red Embroidered Shoes

"All night the bee clung, trembling, to the pistil."
Huang O, 1519, with her new husband.
Her father, a Ming official, ran the Board of Works
and the Ming court permitted art erotic to flourish . . .
"All night the cock's crest stood erect, gorgeous."
She won prizes for poems. Nothing is said about her feet.

An obedient daughter, our hero Huang O put her feet
where they belong. "Your lips teased the pistil
of the lotus." Scholars, reading her work, get a gorgeous
hard-on. Huang O rests her ankles on her husband's
shoulders, the lotus hooks tease his ears, a flourish
of the jade zither and presto—everything works

like blazes, like you wouldn't believe! Everything works
for the elongation of the Dynasty. Van Gulik, on feet:
After the Sung there were fewer dancers. And a flourishing
trade in the tiniest slippers. "A bullet from his pistol
struck down the female Mandarin duck." Husbands
could run around. For them ugly feet were a gorgeous

advantage. The beggar women had big, gorgeous
feet, but they starved. They worked the streets, worked
for officials if they were lucky. Huang O got a husband,
ate Peking duck, the root of lotus. Her feet
measured three inches. Now the red shoes. Pistol
at the temple. The Ming Dynasty flourishes,

like all dynasties, at a price. And poetry flourished
for the erotic pleasure of upper class men. Gorgeous,
the erect clitoris waits. Wanton as the pistil
of the orchid. Huang O's mother, on her knees, worked
the bandages tighter, while the father watched. The feet
stink, but daughter needs must get a husband

or die of shame. Understand it's not her husband's
doing. Though in due time his daughter too flourished.
"My lover draws the silk stockings over my feet,
perfumed with orchids." The poetry, you agree, gorgeous—
and has survived the centuries. Sons become fathers, work
for the Court. "Every night you make blossom pistols

of fire." Husband, that's a gorgeous Board of Works
you've got there. The pistols of the Red Army a flourish
in the future. Huang O, I kneel, I wash your feet.

(Quotations are from Huang O's poems in The Orchid Boat, *translated and edited by Kenneth Rexroth and Ling Chung.)*

Passage

The unicorn
stands beneath the palm. White
the heat, and there is no sound
in the sand. The unicorn does not
move. The palm has four fronds.

Thick the palm's
trunk, and slender the flanks
of the unicorn. A pool reflects the sky
where one cloud drifts. It is evening
of the fifth day.

I can see
the plumes of the palm fronds,
and the unicorn's mane,
tiny ringlets. For the first time
I hear the flute.

I have left home
for good. Surely the throat is a powerful
muscle and the unicorn's horn spiraling
fire. You hear the thunder
of my approach. Behind me

the desert I have crossed.

The Muse And Her Instrument

She holds the blue three-crescent standard, unfurling
I bear the wounds for her

She lifts the blue torch
I carry the bowl of blood in the pelvis

She is the lightning streak
I am the dazzled ground

She is the cool shell of the robin's egg
I am heat woven in the nest

She is a ribbon in the hair
I am the rose at the waist

With her right hand she holds the sky
Below I rock the lava

She is the wind's insignia stitched to the stranger's shoulder
I am the firebrick of the oven floor

She looks out from the eyes of my children
She floats in the bowl of violets
She lays her hands like dusk on my burning hair

She is the thin, blue thread of the flute
I am the thud of the blood drum

She is the vein, I am the artery
circling, circling, circling

Even the red horses, the blue horses
can't tear us apart

She Speaks A Various Language

The floor is cold
the ground frozen
This is the bottom
All the world's seeds have wound down

And just when the stem of my spine
seems to have dried up
and become a stalk
on which my head merely nods

just when I think nothing is left alive

the bare branches of the trees
rise up, beckoning

And it isn't simply
that I want to go out to them
They also want me to come

Come, they say in their motion
in their scraping of branch against branch
like a woman rubbing her hands together

Come with us   where we are going
Walk with us   up into the wind

Peoples' Republic of China:
The No. 1 Machine Tool Factory Foreman's Wife

The bitter day comes down. What can I say—
that I saw your face, they let me look
at you? The wind blew, and then the wind
died down. It didn't rain, and then again
it rained. (Everyone wants his corner on the truth.)
The sun ran, in the usual way, its course.

Love runs its course in secret here. Of course,
good reasons. Say marriage keeps it simple. Say
the State first feeds a billion people. True.
Love later, maybe. We are poor. Don't look
at her, you can't afford it. Don't ask again.
Serve the people. Walk into the wind

and keep on walking. I walk the billowing wind
with you, any excuse: need bread, of course,
need grain (so do the masses). Go out again,
buy tickets for the train. "This time," you say,
"is precious." (Yes, and going fast. It looks
like rain.) Your look tells me a lovely truth,

and walking's a room where we can speak the truth
nakedly. A room we make together. The wind
pours down. We walk to be alone, the course
of our lives one course, here on the street. You say
"I love you." The crowds stream by, you say it again—

time careening, rain beginning—and again.
Around us the masses mass. They are the truth
we have to live with. A Marxist must, so say
the papers. You take my hand anyway, the wind
goes wild, and time is all we have. Of course
it's right to serve the people. Marxists must look

ahead. Put thy shoulder to the present, and look
not back at me. A truth come round again
with poignant vengeance. The people must of course
be fed, love is a luxury. We are the truth
we have to live with, but they are many. The wind
dies down. (You can't have everything.) The papers say

a Marxist must be sober. Say truth: of course
we kissed. Once. In the wind. Oh drunken Marxist,
look in my eyes once more and drink again.

Demeter

Heat, and whirr of insects

With night still in our mouths
we are fatally innocent,

rocked through dark in the body of earth,

lulled
by her sustained agony
and the bredth of her coma.

Matriphobia

I was what you could call critical of my mother.
I attacked her ways every chance I got—
the length of her dresses, the line of her lipstick,
how she drank coffee and the too round roundness
of her belly, especially this. You were
not supposed to have a belly then—I'd determined
never to have one—but my mother did and she seemed
to flaunt it, at least she didn't pretend
it wasn't there,

                                        and there it was.
Squares, rectangles and cubes are invincible
but a sphere looks like a chance to break in.
Roundness invited target practice
and I did not want it around me.
I tried to refute the existence of ovals,
turned my back and broke the eggs
myself. I took a tray to my room
every evening that winter, and left her alone
at the table with my father.

One day, passing a mirror, I saw:
this was the way, passing a mirror,
she stood. All that winter
had been in vain. I resolved then
to train myself out of her body
the way an athlete trains against an opponent's
record. I worked to change the way
I walked and stood and sat. Ate meat again
but not the fat—I'd by god keep my belly
FLAT—

and I would change the world myself
since she had failed to change it for me.
In Randall's Department Store, trying on
my first bikini ever, I looked in the mirror:
my breasts were not so obvious as hers,
but I knew they would be, oh in due, due time
they would be! I slumped onto the beige
plush, and wept. There was to be
no escape for me ever. I too
was lush. I looked just like her.

Only the defeated know how it feels
to rise anyway. I stood up, got dressed,
bought that bikini, and I walked out of there
and threw myself into her: I became her,

the woman I am today. Today,
stepping out of the shower, my daughter, brushing
her hair, glances askance at my persistent
parts. I know
what she's thinking: evolution
is a failure and here
we are, inhabiting the same frame
at the same time. With a gesture of dismissal,
snapping her hair to the side the way a horse
switches its glorious tail, glad
to be going, she walks out

hoping to leave me behind. Her father,
that handsome foreigner, agrees to drive her
to *The Denver.* He's partial to this daughter
and admires my mother more than is called for.
He knows a good thing when he sees one,
and if one is as good as I am

more of us is sure to be better. These two
are just more of me, the woman
he fell in love with.
Sweet fool that he is,
he believes this.

Poem At 5:05 In The Morning

I hear the clock
stop. Winter,

streaming, spiral arms of the galaxies,
cold works. The tick

of the atom
and the children

pulsing, small timers,
pumping the second hand

in the heart. Blood
a high hum

and a low buzz,
the nerves, the nerve

ends. I string some words
on a thread, another

and another, everything still
swings in its arc,

all of us
easy in harness

pulling the light.

Sestina Rima: She Laments Her Rotten Luck

for Peter

Rain drums its dirge on the portico's gray
canopy, and I whine and moan. I miss you.
I do not want to wile the hours away.
I care not what happens or doesn't without you.
The piano twirls merrily above.
I don't make love.

The statuary have been bound and gagged for the winter,
and the amplifier's broken. Sunday afternoon. No mail
today. I feel like a character forced into a Pinter
play against my will. No cakes and ale
and no one is nibbling my thigh.
Time does not fly.

I ought to aspire to a busy and productive independence.
I ought to be racking up a helluva score.
I ought to get dressed. I ought to get up. But what a nuisance
to be beautiful for the creep on the seventh floor.
Remind me not to leave again.
I guess you win.

Drawing

The white paper
is beautiful

all by itself. Now a single
crayon. Say red. Say

green. She
sits on the grass, the boy

beside her. They have paper, color,
light. They want

for nothing. And their mother
will come, bend down, exclaim,

skirt a spray of sequins
cast on the grass, and their father

in a suit, tobacco in the pocket,
will kiss their hair—though there are

those who need their Scotch,
their fast cars, their furs,

all it really takes to be happy
is a couple of crayons,

some plain white paper,
and the absence of the sound

of approaching planes
until it gets too dark to see.

Silverware

A bouquet of silverware on the counter, scattered, someone is leaving. Someone about to pack these forks and spoons in their carved box, a woman has run out into the street to pull her boy back from the deadly flash of chrome. Now she gathers him against her apron, and he feels her fear ticking beneath the meadow of her apron, that ticking the counting of many leavings, as many as there are blades of grass. He remembers rooms left empty, rooms that hold their emptiness like his mother held herself with her own crossed arms in the room where his grandfather's thread was cut and for the second time he saw her cry, as she cried the first time when a tall man in boots, oiled with an oil that smelled like the bears at the zoo, put down his fork, pushed back his chair, and walked out of the room.

We are born with our mouths empty, we are born with a thread fine as a grass blade in the palm of the hand. Low light scatters across the grass like a handful of silver, spoons you can see your face in, your own face curving toward you to embrace you, your last embrace. And the forks, which one evening we lay down for the last time. *You should be used to this by now,* the woman tells herself. But she can't get used to the flash of a chrome fender like a scythe blade, a scissors, or the light pricking her shoulders like the tines of a silver fork.

The forks and spoons lie where they have fallen. Things lie where they fall. Now she winds their long thinnesses in linen, lays them in the pine box. They will lay in a row, gleaming, a swath of cut grass, they will lay like the Pharaohs' bones in the boats carved to carry them to the other world. In the van en route to Thermopoli, Wisconsin, these spoons and forks will sleep on the one, long curve of the current, on this last floating away from the shore which is crumbling, the bank washing away grain by grain, dust to dust.

Someone is leaving. Every day we wrap a spoon in linen, lay it in the bottom of the boat, cut the thread and heave it, with a breath, into the current. Someone is folding the last fold, someone is winding the linen one last turn, someone is going out the door, closing the door like the lid of a carved box. And now the boy sees in the palm of his hand that thread his mother has given him to unwind, this strand strung one after another with leavings, each one ticked off, as though clipped with a scissors, a second of pain, and he is full of rage, and afraid. How he wants to give it back to her, this thread that links him to the shore that is crumbling, this mouth aching for the spoon, this life in which over and over we pick up a fork and begin again, and he presses the palm of his hand against her apron where the root of each blade of grass is beating, beating, beating like a tiny heart. But his small hand is only a faint print on the meadow. The flattened grass will rise again, reaching for light.

Dear Tomato

for Michael

My grandmother always prayed
before eating. I thought she was talking
to God, and maybe
she was. But today I thought of her phrase
Bless this food, and I finally
got it: you can address Him directly,
ask after the Hereafter, but when you say
Bless this food, you are using Him
to speak to the things of this world.

Squirrel, I mutter. Quince bush. Sun-going-down.
I think of all those vocabulary lists
we had to master in grade school. Tree,
mountain, hedgehog. Papaya. Was I praying?

I sit down at the table. It seems important now
to talk to the food. Keep up my half
of the conversation. I try just saying
the names of things. *Tomato. Good bread.*
Parsley. I feel good, and the words
sound right. God is nowhere in sight.

Now that I think of it,
though my grandmother was a Presbyterian
and spoke with her Lord on a regular
basis, hoping for a progress report on the universe,
I'll bet she knew, when she said
tomato, who it was
she was talking to.

Snapshot, Tianjin, 1982: The Extended Sestina

March: the Institute grounds. Behind us the gate
to the foreigners' compound. Your face is the lotus, Romola,
early open, and I am beside you. Those men
in blue are building the Workers' Paradise. More afternoons
this mild, I thought, could get me through. We stand
in the wind, student with teacher, mother with daughter.

I was very nearly what you'd always wanted in a daughter,
I who read Shakespeare and laughed in the classroom. That gate
was locked by Red Guards in the Sixties. Here where we stand
the Brigade made you stand alone, the name *Romola*
a scarlet *A* black across your bosom. This afternoon
low wind, over water, lifts your letter. Those men

were young and idealistic, bitter and old. Those men
who belonged to The Party they wouldn't let you join.
Your daughter, seven, said you were a spy. "Afternoon,
and I listen to your voice on the tape: I watch the gate
but you don't come. I have no one to talk to." Romola,
George Eliot wasn't her real name either. I stand

on another continent as you speak: "Now I can't stand,
my left eye won't open." When you were pardoned, the men
made you teach Marxism—Leninism. (You, Romola,
knew sixteen arias by heart.) Now your daughter
works for the oil men and despises the sonnet, that gate
to your heart's compound. She was fourteen the afternoon

they brought you back—the shafted light of noon's
bright canopy over you both—and she cursed you. Stand,
recite Hamlet's soliloquy. English is the gate
to Shakespeare, George Eliot, laughter, the language of men
who are kind, you suppose, to each other—and I am their daughter,
everything you want but can't have. Romola,

that winter—remember? It was pig iron and steel, Romola,
metal. *Nothing will grow here.* That afternoon
your face was the first loveliness. (A daughter
may say so, especially when she's lonely.) Understand
I had come expecting beauty. The officials, men
in uniform, flanking that gate—now look: the gate's

ajar, as though we'll both go—and through that gate
I walked, finally, away from you. Romola,
here for better or worse is my home. Men
in dark blue wait for the sun to go down. Afternoon
here is evening of the next day there. You stand
in that wind, waiting: the gate's open, but your daughter—

your daughter the drilling rig driver—doesn't come.
The men stand, close the gate: another afternoon, gone.
Romola, I'm afraid I'll never see you again.

Grandmother

I wasn't there when your body, signaling, woke you
When you sat, moving yourself to the edge, and stood
and knew July by its heat and wondered what time it was
and steadied yourself, sat down, and called out for my mother

When she came, her impatience visible in the air around her
because it was hot and something in a pot needed stirring
When she helped you into the slip worn thin by your patience
When she asked which dress you wanted to wear

and when you pulled on the stockings yourself, and the garters
and stepped into your shoes and looked down and knew
and did not tell my mother you knew
When you asked her please would she comb your hair

When you sat down to the meal with my mother and father
and my father asked *would you like some of this and some of this*
When you lifted the glass and gazed through the water's prism
When you drank, swallow by swallow, all of the water

and opened the napkin but did not pick up the fork
When you folded the napkin and pushed back the plate,
pushed back the chair and stood with no help from anyone
and turned, saying nothing, and walked out of the room

When they called you   When you did not answer
When you shut the door and looked at your face in the mirror
Your face, that friend of long standing, that trustworthy sister
When you took this face in your hands to bid it goodby

and when you said to them *I want to lie down now*
When they laid you down and covered you with a sheet
and you said *Go on now, go eat* and they did
because they had worked and were hungry and this had happened
before

When you lay back in it to let it have you
knowing what you had waited for patiently and impatiently
what you had longed and hoped for and abandoned longing and
hoping for
and prayed for and not received was finally here

When you lay back in it to let it have you
When you heard for the last time the clink of silver
and let go the sheet, let go light on the earth
When your breath ceased to be a thing that belonged to you

I wasn't there
Forgive me
I wasn't there

Peoples' Republic of China: The Open Ended Sestina

I begin to miss you long, long before my leaving.
Time turns into a substance with texture, thin
when you're gone (is *this* how I will feel?), dazzling
veils of gossamer light opening into clarity
when you're here. (Exaggeration? No. Information. I handle
reality as closely as I can.) Now the petals open

more, and I am no longer afraid to open
my hands. Yes, this is a love poem, leaving
out words that will flare, burn. I've learned to handle
the impossible like fire—dance around it. "You're thin,
eat more." You spoke in code, there where the clarity
of accuracy was anathema. (I was robust—dazzling—

and both of us knew it.) On the table a glass of water, dazzling
in the light. Which was always fading. You wanted to open
my mouth with your tongue, speak truth with all the clarity
love brings to language. I said, "I will." Leaving
the beach, I picked up a shell, flesh pink, so thin
light shone through. Another kind of code. "Handle

with care," I said, back in the city (and you handled
me so, even when what happened between us—dazzling
us both—became a strain on the impossibly thin
possibility of action). I held out the shell. "Open
your hand—quick now." Then the car came. Leaving,
I let myself turn and look back. Friend, clarity

stuns: I saw your quivering mouth, that clarity
of words you dared not say. Burning, I handle
these words as though they constitute your body. Leaving
your country was easier thanks to the long dazzling
of the breath. From you I learned how full the open
hand is, how love's transparency is never thin

but like a glass of water, opens the thinning
light like a fan. Your face, *the very clarity*
of heaven, looked on my leaving. (Customs. "Open
your luggage." I had everything, and nothing to hide.) We handle
each other in the immense, widening spill of the dazzling
world: wherever I am, you're around. Leaving,

I stay where you are, dazzling that northern air

Incarnate

for Charlie

The day I heard you'd died, that day, toward evening, I was alone in the house, and I turned on the radio. What was there was music, a quiet jazz, sound to sway the body, and then I was dancing. Dancing alone, in that circle we call the spirit, that singular turning, that ceremony of one. I was alone, but I was not alone. I felt someone watching.

The body knows what's right and does that, if you let it. I began to undress then, doing it without thinking, turning, circling, alive on a strand of sound. I was unbound—as though a hand, reluctant, had let go of me. As though unwinding from myself one long strip of bleached linen.

Grief feels like a pulling apart of the net to let a soul fly out. We have to let the dead go. Maybe the dead have to let us go too. Dancing in my own skin at some point I understood: this was you releasing me, you giving me up, giving me back, returning me to my own flesh, its sweetness. You, who had once pointed out to me my own body, the way one child will hand another some treasure—a branch, a leaf, a stone—and say *Here, look at this. Hold this, feel this.*